Sinfully Sweet Cannabis
Recipes
75 Yummy Easy to Make Desserts

By

Rick Butler
Jenny Butler

Published by:
www.Valenciapub.com

Valencia Publishing House
P.O. Box 548
Wilmer, Alabama 36587

Cover & Interior designed

By

Alex Lockridge

First Edition

CONTENTS

INTRODUCTION

Some people want to enjoy the benefits of cannabis without having to smoke it. There are ways you can still get the medical benefits of your cannabis. Have you ever considered cooking with cannabis? The number of recipe options are nearly endless. I'm going to get started by telling you how you can cook with marijuana and then I'm going to give you some of my top recipes for cannabis dessert that I'm sure you'll enjoy.

If you eat cannabis straight without any preparation it not only won't work, but it will also taste pretty bad. Since the digestive system can digest THC directly, you will need to heat it in some way to properly prepare it. It is important to use fat when cooking with cannabis; such as oil, butter or milk. This is because THC is fat soluble and not water soluble. The first step in cooking with cannabis is determining how much THC dosage you are going to put in your recipes.

In our opinion, the most potent way to consume Marijuana is via cooking, especially if you mix it with sugar. But remember once you consume the food, it will take around 90-120 minutes before the THC kicks in, so give it some time and sit back and enjoy the new high of delicious desserts. The good thing about consuming and enjoying it this way is that you don't waste anything, you don't burn anything. It is clean, great tasting and the high time stays longer for you to enjoy.

FROM DRIED WEED TO DESSERT

HOW TO CALCULATE A THC DOSAGE FOR RECIPES

The first step is to determine the percentage of THC in the strain you will be cooking with. On average most strains have 10% THC. A strain of 15-20% are above average, and those with 21% or higher are exceptionally high. If you can't find the online plant breeding info or cannabinoid lab tests for your particular strain, then you should just estimate at 10% THC.

You'll start out with a quarter ounce or seven grams. An eighth is 3.5 grams. Since a gram of cannabis bud has about 1,000 mg of dry weight. Therefore, if a strain has 10% THC, ten percent of 1,000 mg would be 100 mg. So when cooking or baking with cannabis at home, it is safe to assume that a gram of cannabis is going to contain at least 100 mg THC.

To determine the amount of THC per serving you'll

need to take just one more math step. Convert the amount of ground marijuana to milligrams and divide it by the recipe yield in order to determine how much THC you are getting per serving.

A good starting dose for those new to cooking with THC is five milligrams per service. If three grams of ground marijuana equals 300 mg THC, then 300 mg divided by the recipe yield (such as a standard 60 cookie recipe) will equal 5 mg per cookie.

If you want to be even more careful with your cannabis cooking, then 1.5 grams of marijuana divided into 60 cookies would give you 2.5 mg a serving.

DECARBOXYLATION

Cannabis is non-psychoactive when it is raw. It only becomes psychoactive when one of two things happens: 1) as the bud dries and ages and 2) when the cannabis is heated. When cooking the plant, more psychoactive compounds are created than through the aging process. If you want to release the full potential of the plant's psychoactive effects, then you first need to take it through a process known as decarboxylation.

This is a long word for a simple process. All that is required is to heat your herb. A little heat to a dried bud results in an unusual chemical reaction. The primary reaction is to transform compounds known as cannabinoid acids into a form that can be used by the body. Cannabinoids are the chemicals within cannabis that will bind it to cells in the body to produce effects. Sometimes you'll see a recipe refer to decarboxylation as activating or decarbing.

WHY DECARB?

If you don't decarb before cooking, then you won't be getting the full psychoactive effect of the herb. When you decarb before cooking you will make sure you're not wasting the psychoactive potential of the THC. Without decarbing your cannabis, you'll be risking losing its potency.

HOW TO DECARB CANNABIS

Decarboxylation is a very easy process. Before you use your cannabis to cook or bake, you want to follow the six easy steps below:

1. Preheat the oven to 240 degrees Fahrenheit.

2. Break up cannabis flowers and buds into small pieces. Start with one ounce, but you can do more depending on how much cooking you'll be doing.

3. Place the pieces in a single layer on a rimmed baking sheet. Make sure there is no empty space on the pan.

4. Bake the cannabis for 30 to 40 minutes, stirring every 10 minutes for even toasting.

5. Once the cannabis is a light to medium brown in color and has dried out, remove from the oven and allow it to cool. When handled it should be crumbly.

6. Pulse the cannabis in a food processor until it is coarsely ground. Store in an airtight container to use as needed to put directly into the recipe.

4 WAYS TO COOK WITH CANNABIS

There are four main ways to cook with cannabis:

1. Cannabis Butter
2. Cannabis Oil
3. Cannabis Coconut Oil
4. Cannabis Flour

CANNABIS BUTTER

The primary ingredient in most cannabis desserts in cannabis butter. When it comes to making marijuana butter, the most important thing to keep in mind is "low and slow." You want to infuse the butter over low heat for several hours and never allow it to boil. This will allow the THC to activate fully without scorching the cannabis.

You should decarb your cannabis before you infuse it with the butter. You can use any type of unsalted butter to infuse with marijuana, although a high-quality butter will give you a much better taste along with the higher degree of potency. This is because high-quality butter has less water and results in a higher yield. The finished butter will have a green tinge as a result of the cannabis.

Equipment:

- ✓ Spatula
- ✓ Stove
- ✓ Large Saucepan/Pot
- ✓ Whisk
- ✓ Large Glass Bowl
- ✓ Strainer/Sieve that fits over the glass bowl
- ✓ Cheese Cloth
- ✓ Plastic Wrap or Airtight Container
- ✓ Knife

Ingredients:

- ✓ 1/4 ounce cannabis buds, finely ground
- ✓ 1/2 cup (one cube) unsalted butter

Cooking Method:

1. Melt the butter on low heat in a saucepan/pot.

2. Add the ground buds a little at a time, stirring in between.

3. Simmer on a low heat for 45 minutes, stirring frequently. You should start to see small bubbles forming on the surface.

4. After simmering, strain the butter into the container to remove the ground buds.

5. Press a spoon against the ground buds in the strainer to squeeze out all the cannabis butter.

Storage:

Using plastic wrap or an airtight container, your cannabis butter will keep in the refrigerator for several weeks or in the freezer for up to six months.

CANNABIS OIL

This is another option for adding cannabis to your recipe.

Equipment:

✓ Stove

- ✓ Heavy Saucepan or Double Boiler
- ✓ Spatula or Stirring Utensil
- ✓ Metal Strainer
- ✓ Spoon
- ✓ Airtight Container

Ingredients:

- ✓ 6 cups olive oil or canola oil
- ✓ 1-ounce cannabis buds, finely ground or 2 ounces trimmed leaf, dried and ground

Cooking Method:

In a heavy saucepan or double boiler, slowly heat the oil on low heat for a few minutes. As you start to smell the oil's aroma, add a little bit of cannabis to the oil and stir until fully coated with oil. Add more cannabis until all is mixed into the oil. Simmer on low heat for 45 minutes, stirring occasionally. Remove the mixture from the heat and allow it to cool. Strain into your container. Press the cannabis against the strainer with the back of a spoon to wring out all the oil.

Storage:

Cannabis oil can be stored in the refrigerator for up to two months.

CANNABIS COCONUT OIL

Cannabis coconut oil is known for absorbing more cannabis than other butters and oils so it can make for a stronger compound to add to your recipes. It is also a little more involved process than the previous two methods we've discussed.

Equipment:

- ✓ Crock-pot
- ✓ Fine Metal Strainer
- ✓ Cheese Cloth
- ✓ Thermometer

Ingredients:

- ✓ 16 oz. Coconut Oil
- ✓ 1-3 ounces of dried marijuana

✓ Water

Cooking Method:

1. Grind the cannabis extremely fine, but make sure it's not too powdery otherwise it'll be harder to strain later.

2. Add the coconut oil to the crock-pot along with enough water to float the oil. Set the dial on high and allow the oil to liquefy.

3. Slowly start stirring in the bud until the mixture is entirely saturated. Add more water if needed.

4. Place a thermometer in the pot and close the lid, monitor until it reaches close to 250 degrees Fahrenheit. Turn the crock-pot to the low setting and stir.

5. Periodically stir the mixture and check to make sure the temperature stays between 250 and 270 degrees. You may need to regulate the temperature by occasionally flipping from low to warm settings. It is important to stay below 320 degrees to avoid

burning off the active ingredient. Periodically you may need to add water to keep the cannabis completely submerged.

6. After 12 to 18 hours, turn off the crock-pot and allow to cool for a while. Double wrap the cheesecloth over your strainer. Place over a large container to catch all the warm liquid. Slowly pour the mixture into the cheese cloth and allow to drip into the container. If it isn't too hot, you can wrap the plant material and squeeze out the hot oil. Continue until all the mixture is squeezed out of the cheese cloth.

7. Place the container of hot oil/water mix into the refrigerator overnight to allow the oil to rise to the top.
8. The hardened green coconut oil will pop off the top of the water that has sunk to the bottom overnight. Discard the water.

Storage:

Store the coconut oil in the refrigerator until you are ready to use. Allow it to warm before you add it to any recipes.

CANNABIS FLOUR

Start by removing all stems and seeds from the marijuana buds. Allow the buds to dry thoroughly, even a slight amount of moisture can result in a paste rather than a powder.

Next, grind the flowers using a food processor or a coffee grinder. The goal is to get a fine powder almost like flour. It may take some time, but you want to keep grinding and blending until almost everything is pulverized.

Sift through the ground material for unground parts. Use a wire strainer or flour sifter over a bowl to separate unground parts from ground parts. There should only be a little bit to none of the unground parts. Set aside the bowl of ground marijuana for now.

Regrind any of the unground parts. If you can't get the unground parts reprocessed in a food processor or coffee grinder, then you should use a mortar and pestle. You can even apply this process to the already ground flour if you find the texture is more to your liking.

You can then store this marijuana flour in an airtight container. The potency of the marijuana is degraded by oxidation if you don't store it appropriately. If you don't have an airtight container, then you can use vacuum sealing. It should be used within 24 hours or stored in a freezer for long term storage.

You can substitute marijuana flour for a portion of the recipe's requirement. Often you will use a 10% substitution, but you can go as high as 20%. This especially applies to baked goods that need to rise such as bread or cake.

TIPS FOR COOKING WITH CANNABIS

When cooking with cannabis, you want to use the same common sense kitchen rules and safety precautions as you would with any other cooking. You should have dedicated pots and utensils when cooking with cannabis, so you don't cross-contaminate anything.

Make sure your kitchen has proper ventilation since cooking with cannabis is a very aromatic process.

When it comes to cooking with cannabis, a good rule of thumb is to start small. Don't start off with a large dose. After you have determined what dose works for you, then you can increase the amount as needed.

When eating your cannabis desserts remember that eating them along with fatty and protein rich foods will cause the effects of marijuana to last longer in the body. When you eat it in a sugar form the high won't last as long. After eating a cannabis edible, it is best to wait two hours and if you don't feel any effects then eat another edible or eat something fatty to increase the effects. If you are feeling too high, then drink orange juice or fruit juice in order to raise your blood sugar and reduce the effects.

Now that I've covered the basics of cooking with cannabis let's get into some of the recipes. You'll be surprised at the number of desserts you can make with cannabis. Find a recipe that sounds yummy and start cooking.

RECIPES

COOKIE RECIPES:

OATMEAL COOKIES

Ingredients:

1 cup softened cannabis butter

1 1/2 cup rolled oats

1 1/2 cup flour

1/2 cup sugar

1/2 cup brown sugar

2 eggs

1 teaspoon salt

1 teaspoon baking soda

1-2 teaspoon vanilla extract

Direction:

➤ Preheat oven to 325 degrees Fahrenheit.

➤ Mix the flour, oats, salt and baking soda in a large mixing bowl.

➤ In a small bowl, mix softened cannabis butter with sugar, brown sugar, eggs and vanilla.

➤ Combine the two bowls, if the dough seems wet or runny then add extra oats and flour.

➤ Use an ice cream scoop to form dough balls and place them on a greased tray or a tray with parchment paper.

➤ Bake for 16 to 18 minutes.

➤ Test by sticking a fork in one of the cookies. They're done when no dough clings to the fork.

Recipe typically makes 22 to 24 cookies.

CINNAMON PECAN SANDIES

Ingredients:

1 cup ground pecans

1 cup cannabis butter

2 cups flour

1/2 teaspoon baking powder

1 tablespoon vanilla extract

1 cup brown sugar

2 teaspoons cinnamon

1/2 cup powdered sugar

Directions:

➢ Cream the cannabis butter and sugar together in a mixing bowl until smooth, while creaming add the vanilla extract.

➢ Sift together the flour and baking powder, gradually add to mixing bowl.

➢ Add chopped pecans.

➢ Cover dough and chill for three to four hours.

➢ Preheat oven to 325 degrees Fahrenheit.

➢ Remove from refrigerator and roll dough into golf-sized balls before gently flattening and placing them on an ungreased cookie sheet.

➢ Bake for 20 minutes or until slightly firm and golden.

➢ Remove from oven and place on cooling rack.

➢ Combined powdered sugar and cinnamon and then dust the cookies.

➢ Allow to cool completely.

SHORTBREAD COOKIES

Ingredients:

8 tablespoons cannabis butter

1 cup flour

1/4 teaspoon salt

1/4 teaspoon vanilla extract

1/4 cup powdered sugar

1/2 cup chocolate chips

Directions:

➢ Sift flour and salt into a mixing bowl and set aside.

➢ Place 6 tablespoons cannabis butter in another bowl and whisk at high speed until light and fluffy.

- Add powdered sugar and mix at medium speed until thoroughly combined.
- Add vanilla extract and continue to beat.
- Add flour and salt mixture with a spoon and beat until it starts to crumble. Continue to beat until it becomes soft.
- Once the dough becomes pliable, form into a ball and place on plastic wrap.
- Roll the dough out into an 8-inch disc and place in the refrigerator for two hours.
- Remove from refrigerator and roll on a nicely floured surface with a floured rolling pin to a thickness of 1/4 inch.
- Use a cookie cutter to cut out the cookies.
- Place cookies on a tray and refrigerate for another thirty minutes.
- Preheat oven to 325 degrees Celsius.
- Bake cookies for 15 minutes until the edges start to brown.
- Remove and place on a cooling rack.
- Use a double boiler and heat water in the bottom pan and place the chocolate chips and 2 tablespoons cannabis butter in the top pan. Stir well until the chocolate and butter are melted and mixed thoroughly. It takes about 10 minutes.

- ➢ Remove sauce from the heat and set aside.
- ➢ Spread powdered sugar on the half cooled cookies.
- ➢ Dip the cookies in the chocolate sauce one at a time and cool.

MACAROONS

Ingredients:

1 and 1/3 cups flaked coconut

1/3 cup sugar

2 tablespoons flour

Salt

Whites of 2 eggs

Vanilla extract

2 tablespoons cannabis butter

Baking chocolate

Directions:

- ➢ Preheat oven to 325 degrees.
- ➢ Grease a large cookie sheet or tray.
- ➢ Combine in a bowl the coconut, sugar, flour and a pinch of salt.
- ➢ Use hands to mix them well and break up any large clumps.

- In a separate bowl, crack the eggs and separate the egg whites.
- Whip the egg whites with a whisk until mixture is shiny and frothy.
- Add the whisked egg whites and vanilla to the dry mixture and combine by tossing with a wooden spoon until light and fluffy.
- Place tablespoon scoops of the mixture on the greased cookie sheet.
- Bake for 15 to 18 minutes or until golden brown.
- Next, place a double boiler on the stove and bring the water to a boil.
- Add the cannabis butter and allow it to melt.
- Add chocolate to the butter.
- Stir until the mixture is glossy.
- Allow macaroons to cool for a few minutes before transferring to a cooling rack.
- Keep the chocolate sauce simmering, so the sauce remains liquid.
- Hold the macaroons from the bottom and dip the tops gently into the sauce.

GREEN TEA SUGAR COOKIES

Ingredients:

2 and 3/4 cups flour

1 teaspoon baking soda

1/2 teaspoon baking powder

1/4 teaspoon salt

2 teaspoons green tea powder, divided

1/2 cup (1 cube) softened unsalted butter

1/2 cup (8 tablespoons) softened cannabis butter

1 and 1/2 cups sugar

1 egg

1 teaspoon vanilla extract

4 tablespoons buttermilk, divided

1 cup powdered sugar

2 tablespoons milk

Directions:

➢ Preheat oven to 340 degrees.

➢ In a medium bowl, whisk together flour, baking soda, baking powder, salt and 1 teaspoon of green tea powder.

➢ In a large bowl combined unsalted butter, cannabis butter, and sugar. Beat on medium speed until fluffy.

- Reduce speed to low and add the egg, vanilla, and 3 tablespoons buttermilk. Beat until well mixed or about one minute.
- Add the flour mixture and mix until combined.
- Form the dough into a ball, wrap in plastic wrap and then refrigerate for an hour.
- Roll pieces of the dough into 1 and 1/2 inch balls and place on an ungreased cookie sheet 2 inches apart.
- Flatten the balls with your hand and brush the tops with the remaining 1 tablespoon buttermilk.
- Bake 8 to 10 minutes or until light golden brown around the edges.
- Remove from the oven and allow to cool for two minutes.
- Transfer to a wire rack to cool completely.
- Allow cookie sheets to cool between batches.
- In a small bowl combine the powdered sugar with the milk and 1 teaspoon of green tea powder, stirring until there are no lumps.
- Brush the glaze onto the cooled cookies.

GINGERBREAD COOKIES

Ingredients:

1/2 cup softened cannabis butter

1/3 cup softened butter

2 1/4 cups flour

2 teaspoons ground ginger

1 teaspoon baking soda

3/4 teaspoon ground cinnamon

1/2 teaspoon ground cloves

1/4 teaspoon salt

1 cup and 2 tablespoons sugar

1 egg

5 tablespoons brown sugar

Directions:

- ➢ Preheat oven to 350 degrees.
- ➢ Grease two cookie sheets.
- ➢ Mix cannabis butter, butter, a cup sugar, egg and brown sugar until combined.
- ➢ Mix in flour, ginger, baking soda, cinnamon, cloves and salt until combined.
- ➢ Roll dough by hand into 1 inch balls.
- ➢ Coat with remaining sugar and place 2 inches apart on cookie sheets.
- ➢ Bake 8 minutes.
- ➢ Allow cooling.

PEANUT BUTTER CHOCOLATE KISS COOKIES

Ingredients:

3/4 cup sugar

1/2 cup packed brown sugar

1/2 cup softened cannabis butter

1/2 cup peanut butter

1 egg

3/4 teaspoon vanilla extract

1/2 teaspoon vanilla extract

1/2 teaspoon salt

1 and 1/2 cups flour or cannabis flour

3/4 teaspoon baking soda

1/4 cup sugar

24 unwrapped Hershey Kisses

Directions:

➤ Beat together 3/4 cup sugar, brown sugar, cannabis butter and peanut butter until light and fluffy.

➤ Add egg, vanilla, and salt; beat until well mixed.

➤ Add flour and baking soda, continue beating until well mixed.

➤ Refrigerate dough for 30 minutes to firm.

➤ Preheat oven to 375 degrees.

➤ Shape dough into one inch-round ball. Roll balls into 1/4 cup sugar and place on ungreased cookie sheet.

➤ Bake for 8 minutes or until very lightly golden brown.

➤ Immediately press a chocolate kiss into the middle of each cookie. Transfer to cooling racks.

➤ Cool for 10 minutes before serving.

CHOCOLATE PEANUT BUTTER NO BAKE COOKIES

Ingredients:

1/2 cup cannabis butter

2 cup sugar

3 tablespoons cocoa powder

1/2 cup milk

1/2 teaspoon salt

3 cups oats

1/2 cup peanut butter

1 teaspoon vanilla extract

Directions:

➢ Lay out 2 two foot long strips of wax paper on the counter.

➢ In a saucepan over medium heat; add cocoa, sugar, cannabis butter, milk, and salt.

➢ Stir until melted and combined.

➢ Turn heat to high, bring mixture to a boil and cook for one minute.

➢ Remove from heat and quickly add peanut butter, vanilla, and oat.

➢ Stir quickly until combined.

➢ Drop tablespoon sized portions on the wax paper.

> ➤ Let stand until hardened.

DOUBLE CHOCOLATE CHIP

Ingredients:

1/2 cup softened cannabis butter

1/2 cup softened butter

1 and 1/2 cups sugar

2 eggs

2 teaspoon vanilla extract

2 cups flour

2/3 cup cocoa powder

3/4 teaspoon baking soda

1/4 teaspoon salt

2 cups chocolate chips

Directions:

- ➢ Preheat oven to 350 degrees.
- ➢ Grease two cookie sheets.
- ➢ Mix cannabis butter, butter, sugar, baking soda, eggs, salt, and vanilla until combined.
- ➢ Add flour and cocoa powder and mix until combined.
- ➢ Add chocolate chips and mix until combined.
- ➢ Roll the dough into 1 inch balls and evenly place 2 inches apart on cookie sheets.
- ➢ Bake 10 minutes.
- ➢ Ideally, serve warm.

CHOCOLATE CHIP COOKIES

Ingredients:

1/2 cup softened cannabis butter

1/2 cup softened butter

2 and 1/4 cups flour

1 teaspoon baking soda

3/4 cup brown sugar

1/4 cup sugar

2 eggs

1 teaspoon vanilla extract

2 cups chocolate chips

Directions:

➢ Preheat oven to 350 degrees.

➢ Grease two cookie sheets.

- ➢ Mix cannabis butter, butter, brown sugar, sugar, baking soda, eggs and vanilla until combined.
- ➢ Add flour and mix until combined.
- ➢ Add chocolate chips and mix until combined.
- ➢ Roll the dough into 1 inch balls and evenly place 2 inches apart on cookie sheets.
- ➢ Bake 10 minutes.
- ➢ Ideally served warm.

TRIPLE CHOCOLATE ESPRESSO COOKIES

Ingredients:

2 cups flour

2/3 cup cocoa powder

2 teaspoons instant espresso powder

1 teaspoon baking soda

1/4 teaspoon salt

1/2 cup (1 cube) softened unsalted butter

1/2 cup (8 tablespoons) softened cannabis butter

1 cup sugar

1/2 cup packed brown sugar

2 eggs

2 teaspoons vanilla extract

1 cup chocolate chips

2/3 cup white chocolate chips

Directions:

- ➤ Preheat oven to 340 degrees.
- ➤ Grease two cookie sheets.
- ➤ Whisk together flour, cocoa, espresso, baking soda and salt in a medium bowl.
- ➤ Combine unsalted butter, cannabis butter, sugar and brown sugar in a separate bowl and beat on medium until fluffy.
- ➤ Reduce speed to low and add the eggs and vanilla. Beat for one minute or until well mixed.
- ➤ Add the flour mixture until combined.
- ➤ Stir in the chocolate chips and white chocolate chips.
- ➤ Drop heaping tablespoons onto the baking sheets 2 inches apart.
- ➤ Bake 7 to 9 minutes or until the cookies are set and no longer shiny.
- ➤ Remove from the oven and let cool for 2 minutes before transferring to a wire rack to cool.

SUGAR COOKIES

Ingredients:

1 cup cannabis butter

1 cup brown sugar

1/2 cup sugar

1 large egg

1 teaspoon vanilla extract

2 cups flour

1/2 teaspoon baking powder

Salt

Directions:

➢ Beat cannabis butter in a large bowl until light and fluffy.

➢ Add sugar a quarter cup at a time while

continuing to beat the mixture.

- ➢ Beat in the egg and vanilla.
- ➢ In a second bowl; mix baking powder, flour and a pinch of salt.
- ➢ Gradually beat the flour mix into the butter mix.
- ➢ Divide the dough into two halves, wrap each in plastic wrap and refrigerate overnight.
- ➢ Roll each half with a rolling pin on a floured surface to a thickness of about 1/4 inch.
- ➢ Use a cookie cutter and place shapes on cookie sheet 1 inch apart.
- ➢ Bake 10 to 12 minutes or until golden brown.
- ➢ Allow cooling.

WHOOPIE COOKIE

Ingredients:

Cake:

3/4 cup brown rice flour

1/4 cup coconut flour

3/4 cup sorghum flour

3/4 cup tapioca starch

1 teaspoon baking soda

1 teaspoon xanthan gum

1/4 teaspoon salt

1/4 cup cocoa powder, divided

1 cup cannabis oil

2 eggs

1 and 1/2 cups sugar

3/4 cup unsweetened applesauce

1 cup buttermilk

1-ounce food coloring

1 teaspoon vanilla extract

Frosting:

1 teaspoon vanilla extract

2 cups powdered sugar

1/2 cup softened cannabis butter

2 packages (8 ounces) softened cream cheese

Directions:

- ➢ Preheat oven to 340 degrees.
- ➢ Grease and flour 2- 9 inch round cake pans.
- ➢ Whisk together the three flours, tapioca starch, baking soda, xanthan gum, salt and three tablespoons cocoa powder in a bowl.
- ➢ Beat cannabis oil and sugar in a large mixing bowl until thoroughly combined.
- ➢ Beat in eggs one at a time until fully incorporated.
- ➢ Stir in applesauce.

- Beat the flour mixture into the wet ingredients, alternating with buttermilk in several additions that begin and end with flour mixture.
- Mix 1 tablespoon cocoa powder with food coloring and vanilla extra in small bowl to make a paste.
- Gently stir paste into the batter.
- Pour batter into the prepared cake pans.
- Bake in oven about 25 minutes or until a toothpick inserted into the center comes out clean.
- Allow the cakes to cool completely.
- Use round cookie cutter to cut out the tops and bottoms of the whoopie cookies.
- Use a frosting bag and cut a bottom corner to pipe the frosting onto one-half of the cake circles.
- Place the other cake half on top.

JAM COOKIES

Ingredients:

1 and 1/2 cup cannabis flour

1/3 teaspoon baking powder

1/3 teaspoon salt

1/2 cup cannabis butter

3/4 cup sugar

1 large egg

1/3 teaspoon vanilla extract

1/2 cup powdered sugar

1 cup strawberry jam

Directions:

➤ Preheat oven to 350 degrees.

- ➢ Mix cannabis flour, baking powder and salt in a bowl and set aside.
- ➢ In a separate bowl, beat together the cannabis butter and sugar until fluffy or about three minutes.
- ➢ Beat in the egg and vanilla.
- ➢ Reduce speed to low and gradually add the flour mixture until combined.
- ➢ Split the dough in half and roll each into a log.
- ➢ Wrap each log in plastic wrap and chill in the refrigerator for at least an hour until firm.
- ➢ Remove from refrigerator and cut dough into 1/4 inch slices. Each log will typically have 20 slices.
- ➢ Place dough on cookie sheet and keep the rest in the refrigerator until ready to bake.
- ➢ Bake for 10 minutes or until edges are golden brown.
- ➢ Remove and allow to cool on wire rack.
- ➢ Allow cookie sheet to cool before baking the next batch.
- ➢ Drop a large teaspoon of strawberry jam on one-half of the cookies and use another cookie on top.
- ➢ Sprinkle the cookies with powdered sugar.

CAKE AND BREAD RECIPES:

BANANA BREAD

Ingredients:

2 cups flour

3/4 teaspoon baking soda

1/2 teaspoon salt

1 cup sugar

1/4 cup softened cannabis butter

3 mashed overripe bananas

2 eggs

3 cups chopped pecans

1/3 cup vanilla yogurt

2 teaspoons vanilla extract

Directions:

➢ Preheat oven to 340 degrees.

➢ Grease 9-by-5 inch loaf pan.

➢ Whisk together the flour, baking soda and salt in a medium bowl.

➢ Beat together the sugar and cannabis butter in a large bowl.

➢ Stir the bananas, eggs, pecans, yogurt and vanilla into the sugar/butter.

- ➢ Add the dry ingredients to wet ingredients until combined.
- ➢ Pour the batter into the loaf pan.
- ➢ Bake 45 to 50 minutes or until light golden brown and a toothpick inserted in the center comes out clean.
- ➢ Let cool for 10 minutes.

CARROT CAKE

Ingredients:

Cake:

4 eggs

1 1/4 cups vegetable oil

2 cups sugar

2 teaspoons vanilla extract

2 cups flour

2 teaspoons baking soda

2 teaspoons baking powder

1/2 teaspoon salt

2 teaspoons cinnamon

3 cups grated carrots

1 cup chopped pecans

Frosting:

1/4 cup cannabis butter

1/4 cup vegetable oil

8 ounces softened cream cheese

4 cups powdered sugar

1 teaspoon vanilla extract

1 cup chopped pecans

Directions:

➤ Preheat oven to 350 degrees.

➤ Grease and flour a 9x13 inch pan.

➤ Beat together eggs, oil, sugar and vanilla in a large bowl.

➤ Mix in flour, baking soda, baking powder, salt and cinnamon.

➤ Stir in carrots.

➤ Fold in pecans.

➤ Pour into the pan. Bake for 40 to 50 minutes or until a toothpick inserted in the center comes out clean.

➤ Allow to cool for ten minutes in the pan and then remove to wire rack to cool completely.

➤ Combine butter, cream cheese, powdered sugar and vanilla in a medium bowl. Beat until smooth and creamy.

➤ Stir in chopped pecans.

➤ Frost the cooled cake.

RUM CAKE

Ingredients:

1 package yellow cake mix

1 package instant vanilla pudding mix

4 eggs

1/2 cup water

1/4 cup cannabis oil

1/4 cup vegetable oil

1/2 cup rum

1/2 cup chopped pecans

3 tablespoons butter

1/4 cup water

1 cup sugar

1/2 cup Rum

Directions:

➢ Preheat oven to 325 degrees.

➢ Grease and flour a 10-inch tube pan.

➢ Combine cake mix and pudding mix.

➢ In a separate bowl; beat eggs, water, vegetable oil, cannabis oil and rum until frothy.

➢ Add cake mix/pudding mix and beat until well mixed.

➢ Spread pecans evenly along the bottom of the

tube pan.

- ➤ Pour batter over the pecans.
- ➤ Bake for 60 minutes or until a toothpick comes out clean when inserted in the center.
- ➤ Cool in pan for 5 minutes then remove, placing immediately in serving dish right side up with pecans on top.
- ➤ During the last 15 to 20 minutes of baking time start to make the glaze.
- ➤ Combine butter, water, and sugar in a saucepan and bring to boil over high heat.
- ➤ Reduce to medium and boil rapidly until thick and syrupy with frequent stirring.
- ➤ Remove from heat and add Rum.
- ➤ While the cake is hot, poke holes in the top with a toothpick.
- ➤ Spoon glaze over the top of the cake.
- ➤ Allow the cake to sit at room temperature for a day before refrigerating.

GERMAN CHOCOLATE CAKE

Ingredients:

Cake:

1/2 cup water

4 (1 ounce) squares of German sweet chocolate

1 cup softened butter

2 cups sugar

4 egg yolks

4 egg whites

1 teaspoon vanilla extract

1 cup buttermilk

2 and 1/2 cups flour

1 teaspoon baking soda

1/2 teaspoon salt

Frosting:

1 cup sugar

1 cup evaporated milk

1/4 cup cannabis butter

3 beaten egg yolks

1 and 1/3 cups flaked coconut

1 cup chopped pecans

1 teaspoon vanilla extract

1/2 teaspoon shortening

1 (1 ounce) square chocolate

Directions:

➢ Preheat oven to 350 degrees.

➢ Grease and flour 3 -9-inch round pans.

➢ Sift together flour, baking soda, and salt; set aside.

➢ Heat water and 4 ounces German chocolate in small saucepan until melted.

➢ Remove from heat and allow to cool.

➢ Cream 1 cup butter and 2 cups sugar in large bowl until light and fluffy.

➢ Beat in 4 egg yolks one at a time.

➢ Blend in melted German chocolate mixture and vanilla.

- ➢ Alternately beat in the flour mixture with the buttermilk; mix just until combined.
- ➢ Beat eggs whites in large bowl until stiff peaks form.
- ➢ Fold 1/3 of the eggs white into the batter, then quickly fold the remaining until no streaks are seen.
- ➢ Pour batter into the 3 prepared pans.
- ➢ Baked for 30 minutes or until a toothpick inserted in the center comes out clean.
- ➢ Allow cooling in pan for 10 minutes before cooling on wire rack.
- ➢ To make the filling: combine sugar, evaporated milk, cannabis butter and 3 egg yolks in a saucepan.
- ➢ Cook on low heat, constantly stirring until thickened.
- ➢ Remove from heat and stir in coconut, pecans, and vanilla.
- ➢ Cool until thick enough to spread.
- ➢ Spread filling between layers and on top.
- ➢ In a small saucepan, melt shortening and chocolate.
- ➢ Stir until smooth and drizzle on sides of cake.

COCONUT CAKE

Ingredients:

1 package yellow cake mix

1 package instant vanilla pudding mix

1 and 1/3 cups water

4 eggs

1/4 cup cannabis oil

2 cups flaked coconut

1 cup chopped walnuts

4 tablespoons melted butter

2 cups flaked coconut

2 teaspoons milk

1/2 teaspoon vanilla extract

1 (8 ounces) package cream cheese

3 and 1/2 cups powdered sugar

Directions:

➢ Preheat oven to 350 degrees.

➢ Grease a 9x13 inch pan.

➢ Combine cake mix, pudding mix, water, eggs, and cannabis oil in a large bowl.

➢ Blend for 4 minutes.

➢ Stir in coconut and nuts.

➢ Pour into prepared pan.

➢ Bake for 30 minutes or until a toothpick inserted in center comes out clean.

➢ Allow cooling.

➢ To make frosting: Melt 2 tablespoons butter over low heat.

➢ Add 3/4 cup of coconut and stir until browned.

➢ Dry on paper towel.

➢ Combine cream cheese and other 2 tablespoons butter.

➢ Alternately add milk and powdered sugar.

➢ Add vanilla.

➢ Stir in remaining 1 and 1/4 cup coconut.

➢ Spread icing on the cake.

➢ Sprinkle with browned coconut.

STRAWBERRY CHEESECAKE

Ingredients:

1 and 1/4 cups graham cracker crumbs

1/4 cup sugar

1/3 cup cannabis butter

2 (10 ounces) packages frozen strawberries, thawed

1 tablespoon cornstarch

3 (8 ounces) packages softened cream cheese

1 (14 ounces) can sweetened condensed milk

1/4 cup lemon juice

3 eggs

1 tablespoon water

Directions:

➢ Combine graham cracker crumbs, sugar, and

cannabis butter.
- ➤ Press mixture into the bottom of an ungreased 9-inch spring form pan.
- ➤ Refrigerate 30 minutes.
- ➤ Combine strawberries and cornstarch in blender or food processor; cover and process until smooth.
- ➤ Pour into saucepan and bring to boil.
- ➤ Stir for 2 minutes.
- ➤ Set aside 1/3 cup sauce to cool. Cover and refrigerate remaining sauce for serving later.
- ➤ Preheat oven to 300 degrees.
- ➤ Beat cream cheese until light and fluffy in a mixing bowl.
- ➤ Gradually beat in milk.
- ➤ Add lemon juice and mix well.
- ➤ Add eggs and beat on low until combined.
- ➤ Pour half of the cream cheese mix over crust.
- ➤ Drop half of the strawberry mixture by 1/2 teaspoons onto the cream cheese.
- ➤ Spoon remaining cream cheese mixture over sauce.
- ➤ Drop remaining strawberry sauce by 1/2 teaspoons on top.
- ➤ Cut through top layer with a knife only to swirl

the strawberry sauce.

- ➢ Bake for 45 to 50 minutes or until center is nearly set.
- ➢ Cool on wire rack for 10 minutes.
- ➢ Run a knife around the edge to loosen then cool for another hour.
- ➢ Refrigerate overnight.
- ➢ Remove side of the pan.
- ➢ Thin chilled strawberry sauce with water and serve with cheesecake.
- ➢ Store leftovers in the refrigerator.

CINNAMON CHEESECAKE

Ingredients:

1 cup graham cracker crumbs

3 tablespoons brown sugar

1 tablespoon cinnamon

1/2 teaspoon nutmeg

5 tablespoons melted cannabis butter

3 (8 ounce) packages cream cheese

1 cup sugar

1 cup sour cream

1 cup heavy cream

3 tablespoons flour

1 tablespoon vanilla extract

3 eggs

Directions:

➢ Preheat oven to 350 degrees.

➢ Combine graham cracker crumbs, brown sugar, cinnamon, nutmeg, and cannabis butter in medium bowl.

➢ Press into bottom of a 9-inch springform pan.

➢ Bake for 10 minutes.

➢ Remove and allow to cool.

➢ Beat cream cheese and sugar in large bowl until smooth.

➢ Beat in sour cream and heavy cream.

➢ Blend in flour and vanilla.

➢ On low speed, add eggs one at a time.

➢ Pour batter over crust.

➢ Bake for 60 to 70 minutes or until center is nearly set.

➢ Refrigerate at least 6 hours or overnight before removing from pan.

PINEAPPLE UPSIDE DOWN CAKE

Ingredients:

Topping:

1/2 cup melted butter

1/2 cup light brown sugar

7 slices of pineapple

1/2 cup maraschino cherries

Cake:

1 and 1/2 cups cannabis flour

1/2 teaspoon baking powder

1/2 teaspoon baking soda

1/2 teaspoon salt

1/2 cup melted cannabis butter

1/2 cup light brown sugar

1/2 cup sugar

2 eggs

1/2 cup milk

1/2 cup pineapple juice

1 teaspoon vanilla extract

Directions:

➢ Preheat oven to 350 degrees.

➢ Start by making the topping: Pour 1/2 cup melted butter into a pie dish, coating the entire pan.

➢ Sprinkle brown sugar on top of the butter.

➢ Lay pineapple slices and cherries on the bottom of the dish.

➢ Set pie dish to the side.

➢ In a large bowl, mix cannabis flour, baking powder, baking soda, and salt; set aside.

➢ In a separate bowl; combine melted cannabis butter, brown sugar and sugar. Whisk until no lumps.

➢ Whisk in eggs, milk, pineapple juice and vanilla until combined.

➢ Slowly add dry ingredients to the mix. Stirring until smooth.

➢ Transfer batter to prepared pan, spreading over

the topic.

- ➤ Bake for 20 minutes uncovered.
- ➤ Remove, cover loosely with aluminum foil and then cook for another 25 minutes or until a toothpick inserted in center comes out clean.
- ➤ Allow cooling for 15 min.
- ➤ Turn pie dish upside down and gently remove cake to a serving dish.

STRAWBERRY SHORTCAKE

Strawberries & Cream:

About 6 pounds of fresh strawberries, although you can use as much as you want.

Whipping cream

1/2 cup sugar

1 teaspoon sugar

Vanilla extract

Directions:

- ➤ Clean strawberries and remove stems.
- ➤ Slice thinly and place in large bowl.
- ➤ Add 1/2 cup sugar and mix into the strawberries.
- ➤ Leave at room temperature for 20 minutes.
- ➤ Mash to the desired consistency.

➤ In a separate bowl, prepare the whipping cream and add a drop or two of vanilla extract to flavor and a teaspoon of sugar.

Shortbread:

3 tablespoons sugar

1 and 1/2 tablespoons baking powder

3 cups flour

3/4 teaspoon salt

1 and 1/2 teaspoons vanilla extract

12 tablespoons of cannabis butter cut into small pieces

1 and 1/2 cups heavy cream

Directions:

➤ Preheat oven to 400 degrees.

➤ In a large bowl combine flour, sugar, baking powder and salt.

➤ Cut the butter into the dry mixture until the butter is pea-sized.

➤ In a separate bowl, combine cream and vanilla.

➤ Make a crater in the center of the flour mixture and pour in the cream mixture.

➤ Mix until dough is evenly moist and well combined while still being a little coarse and dry.

- Only mix ingredients until just combined otherwise overmixing can lead to tough dough or flaky shortcakes.
- Knead dough five times to create a loose ball.
- Place dough on a lightly floured surface.
- Shape it into an 8-inch square that is about an inch thick.
- Cover a cookie sheet with parchment and place the doubt on it then cover it with plastic.
- Place the dough in the refrigerator to chill for 20 minutes.
- Remove and cut the dough into 9 even squares.
- Place squares 2 inches apart on the baking sheet and bake until a light golden brown.
- Stack the biscuits on a plate and add as much strawberries and whipped cream as you want or create a stack with alternating layers.

FLOURLESS CHOCOLATE CAKE

Ingredients:

1/2 cup water

1/4 teaspoon salt

3/4 cup sugar

2 cups chocolate chips

1 cup softened and cubed cannabis butter

6 eggs

1 teaspoon vanilla extract

1/8 cup powdered sugar

Your choice of fresh fruit

Directions:

> Preheat oven to 300 degrees.
> In a saucepan; combine the water, salt, and sugar.
> Over medium heat, stir until sugar is dissolved and then remove from heat.
> In a separate bowl, melt the chocolate chips slowly in the microwave.
> Add the cannabis butter to the melted chocolate and beat well.
> Add hot sugar water and beat well.
> Add eggs one at a time and beat well each time.
> Stir in vanilla extract.
> Pour batter into a greased cake pan.
> Bake for 30 minutes or until a crust has formed on the top of the cake.
> Remove and let it cool in pan for 5 minutes.
> Place on wire rack to finish cooling.
> Dust with powdered sugar.

- ➤ Garnish with fresh fruit as desired.
- ➤ Leftover cake should be stored in the refrigerator in an airtight container.

RED VELVET CAKE

Ingredients:

Cake:

2 and 3/4 cups flour

1 and 3/4 cups sugar

1 teaspoon baking soda

2 teaspoons cocoa powder

2 large eggs at room temperature

3/4 cup cannabis oil

3/4 cup canola oil

1 and 1/4 cup buttermilk

2 teaspoons red food coloring

1 teaspoon vanilla extract

1 tablespoon white vinegar

Frosting:

16 ounces cream cheese

4 ounces slightly softened butter

3 cups powdered sugar

2 teaspoons vanilla extract

Directions:

Cake:

➢ Preheat oven to 325 degrees.

➢ Place parchment on the bottom of 3 8-inch pans.

➢ Combine all dry ingredients and set aside.

➢ Beat eggs slightly.

➢ Add all wet ingredients together.

➢ Mix wet ingredients into the dry ingredients.

➢ Pour batter into prepared pans.

➢ Bake 30 to 35 minutes.

➢ Remove and cool for 5 minutes then place on a wire cooling rack.

Frosting:

➢ Beat butter until soft.

➢ Add cream cheese and mix; scrape bowl occasionally.

➢ Beat until light; slowly add the powdered sugar

and allow it to get completely combined along with some air before adding more.

➢ After all the powdered sugar is combined beat a few minutes before adding vanilla.

➢ Beat again and then ice cake immediately.

OREO COOKIE CAKE

Ingredients:

Cake:

1 package devils food cake mix

1 package instant chocolate pudding mix

1 teaspoon salt

1 teaspoon vanilla extract

1 cup sour cream

1 cup cannabis oil

4 eggs

1/2 cup warm water

2 cups chocolate chips

Frosting:

2 cups room temperature cannabis butter

1 tablespoon vanilla extract

1 and 1/2 pounds powdered sugar

3-4 tablespoons very cold coconut milk

25 chopped Oreo cookies

Directions:

Cake:

➢ Preheat oven to 350 degrees.

➢ Line the bottom of 2 9-inch round cake pans with parchment and grease thoroughly.

➢ Mix the cake mix, pudding mix, salt, vanilla, sour cream, cannabis oil, beaten eggs and water in a large bowl.

➢ Stir in chocolate chips.

➢ Divide batter into the prepared cake pans.

➢ Bake for 25 to 35 minutes, rotating pans halfway through. Bake until the top is springy to the touch and a toothpick inserted in the center comes out clean.

➢ Allow cake to cool for 30 minutes before inverting and cooling on a wire rack.

Frosting:

➢ In a bowl, cream the cannabis butter.

➢ Add vanilla extract and combine well.

➢ Add in the sugar gradually and mix thoroughly every time.

➢ Add the very cold milk one tablespoon at a time, combining well each time.

➢ Fold in chopped Oreo cookies.

➢ Frost your cake layers.

COFFEE CAKE

Ingredients:

Crumb Topping:

2/3 cup light brown sugar

1 tablespoon flour

2 teaspoon cinnamon

1/4 cup cold and diced butter

1 cup chopped and crushed pecans

Cake:

1/2 cup softened cannabis butter

1 cup sugar

2 eggs

2 cups cannabis flour

1 teaspoon baking powder

1/2 teaspoon baking soda

1/4 teaspoon salt

1 cup sour cream

1 teaspoon vanilla extract

Directions:

➢ Preheat oven to 350 degrees.

Topping:

➢ Mix together the light brown sugar, flour, and cinnamon.

- ➢ Add butter and use hands to form a crumb mixture.
- ➢ Mix in pecans and set aside.
- ➢ Cream cannabis butter and sugar in a bowl.
- ➢ Add eggs and beat until light and fluffy.
- ➢ In a separate bowl; mix the cannabis flour, baking soda, baking powder, and salt.
- ➢ Slowly add the dry mixture to the wet ingredients, alternating with the sour cream.
- ➢ Continue mixing until the batter is smooth.
- ➢ Stir in vanilla extract.
- ➢ Pour batter into a greased cake pan.
- ➢ Sprinkle the crumb mixture over the top.
- ➢ Bake for 40 to 45 minutes or until a toothpick inserted in the center comes out clean.
- ➢ Allow cooling 5 to 10 minutes before serving.

BLACK BOTTOM CUPCAKES

Ingredients:

Cheesecake:

1 cup cream cheese

1 egg

1/3 cup sugar

1 teaspoon vanilla extract

1/8 teaspoon salt

1 cup chocolate chips

Cupcakes:

1 and 1/2 cups cannabis flour

1 cup sugar

1/4 cup cocoa powder

1 teaspoon baking soda

1/2 teaspoon salt

1 cup water

1/3 cup vegetable oil

1 tablespoon white vinegar

1/8 cup powdered sugar

Directions:

➢ Preheat oven to 350 degrees.

➢ Lightly grease muffin tin.

➢ Mix cream cheese, egg, sugar, vanilla extract, and salt together.

➢ Stir in chocolate chips and set aside.

➢ In a separate bowl; sift together the cannabis flour, sugar, cocoa, baking soda, and salt.

➢ Add water, oil, and vinegar to the flour mixture and mix until well combined.

➢ Fill each muffin cup 1/3 full with the cocoa batter.

➢ Drop one spoonful of cream cheese mix into the

center of each cup.

➤ Bake for 30 to 35 minutes.

➤ Allow cooling for 5 minutes before removing from pan.

➤ Sprinkle with powdered sugar.

CHOCOLATE CAKE

Ingredients:

3/4 cup cannabis oil

1 pack dark chocolate cake mix

3 eggs

1 box chocolate instant pudding

2 cups cold milk

1 tub chocolate frosting

Directions:

- ➢ Preheat oven to 400 degrees.
- ➢ Make the cake batter according to package directions, substituting the cannabis oil for the regular oil.
- ➢ Mix it with eggs and water.
- ➢ Pour the cake mixture into 2 evenly sized cake pans.
- ➢ Bake for 30 minutes or until a toothpick inserted in the center comes out clean.
- ➢ Make the pudding mix.
- ➢ Spread the pudding mix over the top of a cake.
- ➢ Place the other cake on the top.
- ➢ Cover the cake with chocolate frosting.

POPPY SEED CAKE

Ingredients:

Cake:

1 and 3/4 cups cannabis flour

1/2 teaspoon baking powder

1/2 teaspoon baking soda

1/8 teaspoon salt

1/2 cup softened cannabis butter

1 and 1/4 cups sugar

3 eggs

1 cup crème fraiche

3 tablespoons poppy seeds

1/2 teaspoon almond extract

Frosting:

4 ounces softened cream cheese

2/3 cup powdered sugar

1 cup crème fraiche

1 teaspoon finely grated lemon peel

1/8 teaspoon almond extract

Directions:

➢ Preheat oven to 350 degrees.

➢ Grease a 9-inch square pan.

➢ Stir together cannabis flour, baking powder, baking soda and salt in a medium bowl.

➢ Beat butter for 30 seconds at medium speed in a large bowl or until creamy.

➢ Add sugar and beat for 5 minutes or until light, creamy and fluffy.

➢ Add eggs one at a time and beat until well blended.

➢ Beat in flour mixture at low speed in 3 parts, alternating with 1 cup crème fraiche. Begin and end with the flour mixture.

- Beat in poppy seeds and 1/2 teaspoon almond extract.
- Spoon and spread the batter into the greased pan.
- Bake 35 to 40 minutes or until dark golden brown and a toothpick inserted into the center comes out clean.
- Cool completely on wire rack.
- In a large bowl, beat cream cheese and powdered sugar on low speed until smooth.
- Slow beat in 1 cup crème fraiche until well mixed.
- Increase to medium speed and beat until firm.
- Beat in lemon peel and 1/8 teaspoon almond extract.
- Spread frosting over cake just before serving or store in the refrigerator.

ROCKY ROAD CAKE

Ingredients:

Cake:

225-gram dark chocolate

225-gram cannabis butter

345-gram caster sugar

6 eggs, separated into yolks and whites

145-gram soft white breadcrumbs

30-gram flour

4 teaspoons vanilla extract

120-gram ground almonds

Icing:

85-gram cocoa powder

225-gram icing sugar

130-gram cannabis butter

6 tablespoons water

170-gram caster sugar

Directions:

> Preheat oven to 160 degrees Celsius.

> Grease and line a 24cm round cake pan.

> In a double boiler, melt the chocolate.

> Cream the cannabis butter with 345-gram sugar until softened and pale.

> In a different bowl, whip the eggs whites with a pinch of sugar until stiff but not dry.

> Fold eggs whites into the cake mix and pour into the cake tin.

> Bake for 1 hour or until firm.

> For the icing, sieve the cocoa and icing sugar into a separate bowl.

> Warm the cannabis butter, water, and sugar in a

microwave or double boiler and simmer until the sugar is dissolved.

➢ Add the liquid to the dry ingredients and stir until thick.

➢ Spread the icing on the cake.

BUTTER POUND CAKE

Ingredients:

1/2 cup softened cannabis butter

1 cup softened butter

1 (8 ounces) softened cream cheese

3 cups sugar

6 eggs

3 cups flour

1 teaspoon vanilla extract

Directions:

➢ Preheat oven to 325 degrees.

➢ Grease a 9x5 bread pan.

➢ Mix everything except the flour until well combined.

➢ Add flour mix until well combined.

➢ Pour mixture into greased pan.

➢ Bake 80 minutes or until a toothpick inserted in the center comes out clean.

➢ Allow cooling before serving.

PUMPKIN CAKE

Ingredients:

1/2 cup melted cannabis butter

1 box yellow cake mix

3/4 cup sugar

1 can pumpkin puree

1/4 cup water

1 teaspoon cinnamon

4 eggs

Directions:

- ➢ Preheat oven to 350 degrees.
- ➢ Grease a 9x13 inch baking pan.
- ➢ Mix everything until well combined.
- ➢ Pour into baking dish.
- ➢ Bake 45 minutes.
- ➢ Allow cooling before serving.

COCOA PUFF CUPCAKES

Ingredients:

1 and 1/2 cups flour

1 cup sugar

1/2 cup cocoa powder

1 teaspoon baking soda

1/4 teaspoon salt

1 large egg

4 to 6 tablespoons cannabis butter

2 and 1/2 tablespoons melted butter

1 teaspoon vanilla extract

1 cup whole milk

1 cup powdered sugar

1 and 1/2 tablespoons milk

3 large handfuls of Cocoa Puffs cereal

Directions:

➤ Preheat oven to 350 degrees.

➤ Grease a muffin tin.

➤ In a large mixing bowl, sift together the flour, cocoa, sugar, baking soda, and salt.

➤ In a separate bowl; whisk the egg together with the cannabis butter, butter and vanilla extract until mixed well.

➤ Add the egg mix to the flour mix and stir until combined well.

➤ Pour the batter into the muffin tin until each cup is about 2/3 full.

➤ Bake 18 to 22 minutes until a toothpick inserted in the center comes out clean.

➤ Allow cooling for 5 to 10 minutes.

➤ Remove from tin and finish cooling on wire rack.

> For the icing, combine powdered sugar and milk in a bowl and top cupcakes.

> Dot the tops with Cocoa Puffs.

CARAMEL CRUNCH BARS

Ingredients:

Cake:

1 and 1/2 cups rolled oats

1 and 1/2 cups flour

3/4 cup brown sugar

1/2 teaspoon baking soda

1/4 teaspoon salt

1/4 cup melted cannabis butter

1/4 cup melted butter

Topping:

1/2 cup brown sugar

1/2 cup sugar

1/2 cup butter

1/4 cup flour

1 cup chopped nuts

1 cup chopped chocolate

Directions:

> Preheat oven to 375 degrees.

- Great a 9x13 inch baking pan.
- In a large bowl; combine oats, brown sugar, flour, salt and baking soda.
- Add cannabis butter and butter, stir until the texture is crumbly.
- Set aside one cup for use later as a topping.
- Press remaining mixture into bottom of prepared pan.
- Bake for 10 minutes or until light brown.
- Remove and cool for 10 minutes, leave the oven on for now.
- While the bars cool, prepare the topping by stirring the sugars and butter in a saucepan.
- Heat over minimal heat until bubbling and then simmer for 30 seconds.
- Remove from heat and cool until lukewarm; stir in flour.
- Place chocolate pieces on top of the oat base.
- Place mixed nuts on the top of the chocolate.
- Drizzle on the caramel topping.
- Place the cup of uncooked oat mix set aside from before on top.
- Bake for another 20 minutes or until they are golden brown.
- Cool and then serve.

PIE RECIPES:

BANANA CREAM PIE

Ingredients:

3/4 cup sugar

3 tablespoons cornstarch

1/2 teaspoon salt

3 cups milk

3 eggs

2 tablespoons cannabis butter

1 teaspoon vanilla extract

1 9-inch pre-baked pastry shell

4 large bananas

1 cup whipped cream

Directions:

➢ In a large saucepan; combine sugar, cornstarch, salt, and milk. Stir until smooth.

➢ Over medium-high heat, heat while constantly stirring until bubbling and starts to thicken.

➢ Reduce heat to low, heat for 2 more minutes then remove from heat.

➢ In a small bowl, beat eggs slightly.

➢ Add 1/2 cup of hot milk to eggs and stir.

➢ Add eggs to the saucepan, stir together.

➢ Increase heat and constantly stir until a slight boil.

➢ Remove from heat then add cannabis butter and vanilla extract, mixing well.

➢ Transfer mixture to a sealed container. Cover and refrigerate for 1 hour.

➢ Spread half of the filling in the 9-inch pastry shell.

➢ Slice bananas and lay on top, covering the entire surface.

➢ Pour rest of the filling over the bananas.

➢ Top with whipped cream.

> Refrigerate for 8 hours before serving.

PUMPKIN PIE

Ingredients:

Filling:

2 eggs

1 cup brown sugar

1 and 1/2 cups pumpkin puree

1 cup cream

3 tablespoons melted and cooled cannabis butter

1 teaspoon cinnamon

1/2 teaspoon nutmeg

1/2 teaspoon ground ginger

1 pie crust

Pie Crust:

2 cups flour

1 teaspoon salt

2 sticks unsalted butter

1/3 to 1/2 cup water

Directions:

Filling:

- ➤ Preheat oven to 350 degrees.
- ➤ Beat the eggs and sugar in a medium bowl until fluffy and light.
- ➤ Add pumpkin, cream, cannabis butter, cinnamon, nutmeg, and ginger; mix well.
- ➤ Pour into pie crust and bake until done.

Pie Crust:

- ➤ Combine flour and salt in a large bowl.
- ➤ Cut in butter until it is coarse crumbs.
- ➤ Stir in water until it forms a ball.
- ➤ Divide in half and shape into balls.
- ➤ Wrap in plastic and refrigerate 4 hours to overnight.
- ➤ Roll dough on a floured counter.

APPLE PIE

Ingredients:

2 sheets of refrigerated pie crusts

6 cups cored, peeled and sliced apples

1 tablespoon lemon juice

1/3 cup brown sugar

1/2 cup sugar

1 and 1/2 cups cubed cannabis butter

1/8 cup flour

1 teaspoon cinnamon

1/8 teaspoon nutmeg

1/2 teaspoon salt

Directions:

➤ Press 1 pie crust firmly into the bottom of a pie dish and up the sides.

➤ Trim the dough edge, leaving 1 inch of dough to hang over the edge.

➤ In a large bowl, combine apples and lemon juice; mix well.

➤ Add brown sugar, sugar, flour, cinnamon, salt, and nutmeg; mix well and ensure all apples are coated.

➤ Transfer filling to the pie crust lined the pan.

➤ Evenly lay the cubed cannabis butter on top of the apple filling.

➤ Place the second pie sheet on top.

➤ Trim edge appropriately to leave 1 inch hanging over the sides.

➤ Fold the edge of the top under the edge of the bottom piece of dough.

➤ Pinch the dough together to seal.

➤ Cut an X across the top center or poke with a fork to allow steam to escape.

➤ Refrigerate for 20 minutes to make the dough firm.

➤ Preheat oven to 375 degrees.

➤ Bake for 1 hour or until crust is golden brown and

filling bubbles.

➢ Transfer to wire rack and cool for 1 hour before serving.

BLUEBERRY PIE

Ingredients:

2 sheets refrigerated pie crusts

5 cups fresh blueberries

1 cup sugar

1/2 cup cannabis flour

1/2 teaspoon cinnamon

2 tablespoons melted butter

1 large beaten egg

1 teaspoon sugar

Directions:

➢ Press one pie crust into bottom and sides of pie pan.

➢ Trim the dough edge, leaving 1 inch of dough hanging over the sides of the pan.

➢ Stir together blueberries, cannabis flour, sugar, butter, egg, and cinnamon.

➢ Transfer filling to the lined pie pan.

➢ Place second pie sheet over pie.

- ➤ Trim edges, leaving 1 inch hanging over sides.
- ➤ Fold the top layer of dough under the edge of the bottom layer. Pinch together to seal.
- ➤ Cut an X in the center of the dough to allow steam to escape.
- ➤ Refrigerate for 20 minutes to firm dough.
- ➤ Preheat oven to 375 degrees.
- ➤ Bake for 1 hours or until the crust is golden brown and the filling bubbles.
- ➤ Transfer to wire rack to cool for at least 1 hour before serving.

PEACH COBBLER

Ingredients:

1/2 cup melted cannabis butter

1 cup cannabis flour

1 and 1/4 cup sugar

1/2 cup brown sugar

1 teaspoon baking powder

1/4 teaspoon salt

2/3 cup room temperature milk

1 egg

Filling:

8 chopped peaches

1/4 teaspoon cinnamon

1/4 teaspoon nutmeg

Directions:

➢ Preheat oven to 375 degrees.

➢ Pour melted cannabis butter into a 9x13 baking dish.

➢ Mix cannabis flour, 1 cup sugar, baking powder, and salt together.

➢ Add milk and egg, stirring until all dry ingredients are moistened.

➢ Pour mixture evenly over the melted cannabis butter and let sit.

➢ In a saucepan over high heat combine peaches, cinnamon, nutmeg, brown sugar and remaining sugar.

➢ Stir constantly until it boils. Pour the hot peaches into the baking dish over the mixed batter.

➢ Bake for 45 minutes.

➢ Done when batter rises and turns golden brown in color.

CHERRY PIE

Ingredients:

2 sheets refrigerated pie crusts

4 cups pitted cherries

1 cup sugar

1/2 cup cannabis flour

1/4 cup melted cannabis butter

1/2 teaspoon vanilla extract

1 teaspoon sugar

Directions:

➢ Press 1 pie crust into the bottom and sides of a pie pan.

➢ Trim the dough edge, leaving 1 inch hanging over the sides.

➢ Stir cherries, sugar, cannabis flour, cannabis

butter and vanilla extract together.

- ➢ Transfer filling to the pie pan.
- ➢ Place the second sheet over the top.
- ➢ Trim edges, leaving 1 inch of dough hanging over the sides.
- ➢ Fold the top edge under the bottom edge of dough. Pinch together to seal.
- ➢ Cut 6 slits in the top of the dough to let steam escape.
- ➢ Refrigerate for 20 minutes to firm dough.
- ➢ Preheat oven to 375 degrees.
- ➢ Bake for 1 hour or until the crust is golden brown and the filling bubbles.
- ➢ Transfer to wire rack and sprinkle with a teaspoon of sugar.
- ➢ Cool for 1 hour before serving.

PECAN PIE

Ingredients:

1 prepared pie crust

3/4 stick unsalted butter

1-2 ounces melted cannabis butter

1 cup packed light brown sugar

3/4 cup light corn syrup

2 teaspoons vanilla extract

Pinch of salt

3 large eggs

2 cups pecan halves

Directions:

➢ Place dough in a 9-inch pie plate and crimp the edges.

➢ Poke some holes in the bottom of the crust.

➢ Refrigerate for 30 minutes.

➢ Preheat oven to 340 degrees.

➢ Whisk brown sugar, corn syrup, vanilla, salt, unsalted butter and cannabis butter until smooth.

➢ Add eggs and pecan halves; beat.

➢ Place filling in pie crust.

➢ Bake 50 minutes to 1 hour.

➢ Cool completely before serving.

FROZEN DESSERTS:

MINT CHOCOLATE ICE CREAM

Ingredients:

2 cup cannabis milk

1 cup half-and-half

1/2 cup sugar

1 tablespoon corn starch

Pinch of salt

2 egg yolks

1 teaspoon vanilla extract

1 teaspoon mint extract

1 cup dark chocolate pieces

Directions:

- ➤ In a large saucepan; combine cannabis milk, half-and-half, 1/2 cup sugar, cornstarch, and salt.
- ➤ Whisk together thoroughly.
- ➤ Cook over medium heat, constantly stirring until it thickens or about 10 minutes.
- ➤ Remove from heat.
- ➤ In a separate bowl, whisk egg yolks while gradually adding 1 cup of the hot liquid from the saucepan.
- ➤ Return mixture to saucepan while constantly whisking.
- ➤ Heat for an addition 2 minutes while stirring constantly.
- ➤ Pour the mixture through a strainer and into a large bowl. Discard solids.
- ➤ Chill in refrigerator for 1 hour, stirring

occasionally.

- ➢ Cover with plastic wrap and chill for 12 to 24 hours.
- ➢ Pour into ice cream freezer container.
- ➢ Stir in vanilla extract and mint extract.
- ➢ Freeze for 3 hours.
- ➢ Remove and stir in dark chocolate pieces.
- ➢ Return to freezer for 6 hours or until firm.
- ➢ Keep at room temperature for 5 minutes before serving.

CHOCOLATE ICE CREAM

Ingredients:

6 ounces chocolate

2 and 1/4 cup custard

1 and 1/4 cup whipping cream, whipped

1/4 ounce cannabis

Directions:

➢ Melt the chocolate in a microwave or double boiler.

➢ Mix the chocolate into the custard.

➢ Fold the whipped cream into the chocolate/custard.

➢ Place the mixture into a plastic container and freeze.

➢ Place at room temperature a few minutes before serving.

PEACH POPSICLES

Ingredients:

1 cup peach puree

1/2 cup cannabis milk

2 tablespoons sugar

1 cup Greek yogurt

1 teaspoon vanilla extract

1/2 cup diced peaches

Directions:

- ➤ Combine the peach puree, cannabis milk, sugar, Greek yogurt and vanilla extract in a large bowl.
- ➤ Stir in diced peaches.
- ➤ Transfer to your choice of Popsicle molds.
- ➤ Freeze for a minimum of 4 hours.
- ➤ Before opening, run molds under warm water to loosen.

LAYERED POPSICLES

Ingredients:

1 and 1/2 cups fresh raspberries

1/4 cup water

1 tablespoon lemon juice

1/4 cup honey

1 cup cannabis milk

1/4 cup plain yogurt

2 tablespoons sugar

1 and 1/2 cups fresh blueberries

1 tablespoon lime juice

Directions:

- In a blender, puree that raspberries, water, and lemon juice.
- Halfway through, add 1/8 cup honey and continue blending until smooth.
- Pour puree through a sieve into a clean bowl and discard seeds or chunks.
- Fill your choice of Popsicle mold 1/3 full with raspberry puree.
- Freeze for 1 hour.
- Mix cannabis milk, yogurt, and sugar together.
- Remove the molds and fill each another 1/3 full with yogurt mixture.
- Freeze for 1 hour.
- In a blender puree the blueberries, 1/8 cup water, and lime juice.
- Halfway through, add 1/8 cup honey and continue blending until smooth.
- Pour blueberry puree through a sieve into a clean bowl and discard seeds or chunks.
- Remove the molds from the freezer and insert the stick through the yogurt layer.
- Fill the shells with the blueberry puree, leaving less than a 1/2 inch at the top.
- Freeze until solid, about 2 hours.
- Before opening loosen by running molds under

warm water.

PEANUT BUTTER - BANANA ICE CREAM

Ingredients:
2 cups cannabis milk

1 cup milk

1/2 cup sugar

1 tablespoon cornstarch

Pinch of salt

4 pureed bananas

1/2 cup peanut butter

Directions:
➢ In a large saucepan; combine cannabis milk, milk, sugar, and cornstarch.

➢ Whisk thoroughly.

➢ Cook on medium while constantly stirring until it begins to thicken, about 10 minutes.

➢ Remove from heat until it is slightly warm.

➢ Pour through a fine strainer into a large bowl and discard solids.

➢ Chill uncovered in refrigerator for 1 hour, stirring occasionally.

➢ Cover with plastic wrap and chill for 12 to 24

hours.

- Pour mixture into a freezer container.
- Freeze for 2 hours or until ice cream starts to firm, but is still soft.
- Stir in banana puree and peanut butter until well distributed.
- Freeze 6 hours or until firm.
- Leave out at room temperature for 5 minutes before serving.

BERRY SHERBET

Ingredients:

5 cups fresh blackberries

2 cups sugar

2 and 1/2 cups cannabis milk

1 tablespoon lemon juice

Directions:

- Blend blackberries and sugar until smooth.
- Pour through a strainer and into a bowl, discard solids and seeds.
- Mix cannabis milk into the puree.
- Stir in lemon juice.
- Pour mixture into a freezer container.

- ➤ Freeze for 3 hours.
- ➤ Set out at room temperature for 5 minutes before serving.

TROPICAL POPSICLES

Ingredients:

2 Mango's peeled and chunked

2 cups vanilla yogurt

4 tablespoons cream of coconut

2-3 tablespoons cannabis coconut oil

3 tablespoons coconut sugar

2 teaspoons coconut extract

Directions:

- ➤ Place all ingredients in a blender.
- ➤ Puree until smooth.
- ➤ Pour into Popsicle molds of your choice.
- ➤ Freeze until firm.
- ➤ Run molds under warm water to loosen before eating.

CHOCOLATE TREATS:

FUDGE

Ingredients:

2 pounds or 7 cups of powdered sugar

1 cup Hershey's cocoa

1 pound (4 sticks) cannabis butter

1 teaspoon vanilla extract

1 cup peanut butter

Directions:

> In a saucepan or double boiler; melt the cannabis butter and peanut butter.

> Add vanilla extract.

> Mix powdered sugar and cocoa in a large bowl.

- ➤ Add melted ingredients and mix well.
- ➤ Press into a flat pan.
- ➤ Refrigerate until firm.

CHOCOLATE PECAN BARK

Ingredients:

8-ounce dark chocolate

2 tablespoons cannabis butter

1/2 cup Grape Nuts cereal

2 tablespoons chopped, unsweetened dried cherries

2 tablespoons golden raisins

1 tablespoon chopped, unsalted pistachios

1 tablespoon unsalted pecan pieces

Directions:

- ➤ Cover your work area with wax or parchment paper.
- ➤ In a medium microwave-safe bowl, place chocolate and cannabis butter.
- ➤ Heat at half power in 30-second intervals until nearly melted.
- ➤ Remove and stir to fully melt.
- ➤ Using a rubber scraper, turn the chocolate onto the parchment.

- ➢ Spread it as evenly as possible.
- ➢ Sprinkle all the toppings and gently press them into the chocolate.
- ➢ Cool completely until the chocolate is set.
- ➢ Break into pieces to serve.

ROCK ROAD FUDGE

Ingredients:

1 cup cannabis butter

2 cups sugar

1 cup milk

1 teaspoon vanilla extract

25 large marshmallows, quartered

1 cup milk chocolate chips

1 cup semi-sweet chocolate chips

1 cup chopped macadamia nuts

Directions:

- ➢ Grease 11x16 cookie sheet with sides.
- ➢ In a large saucepan; combine sugar, milk, vanilla and cannabis butter.
- ➢ Bring ingredients to boil while stirring occasionally.
- ➢ Boil for 2 minutes and then remove from heat.
- ➢ Add chocolate chips and stir until melted completely and smooth.
- ➢ Add marshmallows and macadamia nuts.
- ➢ Pour into a cookie sheet and refrigerate until solid.

CANDY

HARD CANDY

Ingredients:

2 cups sugar

1 and 1/4 cup cannabis corn syrup

1 cup water

Food coloring and/or flavoring of your choice

Directions:

- ➤ In a saucepan over medium heat; heat sugar, cannabis corn syrup, and water.
- ➤ Stir until all sugar is dissolved.
- ➤ Bring to a 300-degree boil.
- ➤ Add coloring and/or flavoring slowly and stir well.
- ➤ Turn off heat, quickly and carefully pour liquid into candy molds of your choice.
- ➤ After it cools completely, remove candy from the mold.

CARAMELS

Ingredients:

1 cup cannabis butter

2 and 1/4 cups brown sugar

Pinch of salt

1 cup light corn syrup

14 ounce sweetened condensed milk

1 teaspoon vanilla extract

Directions:

- ➤ In a saucepan, slowly melt cannabis butter.
- ➤ Stir in brown sugar and salt until thoroughly combined.
- ➤ Stir in light corn syrup.

- ➤ Add milk slowly and stir constantly.
- ➤ Cook on medium heat until candy starts to get firm, about 12 to 15 minutes.
- ➤ Remove from heat and stir in vanilla extract.
- ➤ Pour into pan and allow for candy to cool.
- ➤ Cut and serve or store in airtight container.

JOLLY RANCHERS

Ingredients:

Big bag of Jolly Ranchers

Cannabis tincture

1/4 cup water

Directions:

- ➤ In a coffee grinder, grind the Jolly Ranchers.
- ➤ Put the ground Jolly Ranchers into the water in a saucepan on the stove.
- ➤ Bring to a temperature of 300 degrees.
- ➤ Remove from heat and add as much cannabis tincture as you want.
- ➤ Pour into candy molds or onto a cookie sheet covered with foil and allow to harden.

GUMMIES

Ingredients:

1/2 cup cold water

1 large packet sugar-free Jello flavor of your choice

4 envelopes gelatin

4 tablespoons cannabis tincture

Directions:

➢ Spray candy molds lightly with oil and wipe with paper towel to leave tiny oil.

➢ Mix Jello and gelatin with a whisk.

➢ Add 1/2 cup cold water and whisk.

➢ Bring to boil and then heat for 5 minutes on low.

➢ Remove from heat.

- ➤ Add 4 tablespoons of tincture and mix well.
- ➤ Pour into molds.
- ➤ Refrigerate for 15 minutes.
- ➤ Peel out of molds.

OTHER SWEETS

COCONUT AND CHOCOLATE MARSHMALLOWS

Ingredients:

2 ounces cannabis butter

2 tablespoons cocoa

3 tablespoons condensed milk

2 ounces brown sugar

6 ounces coconut

5 ounces small white marshmallows

Directions:

- ➤ Melt cannabis butter in a pan.
- ➤ Mix in cocoa, milk, and sugar.
- ➤ Stir occasionally while continuing to heat until everything is melted together.
- ➤ Remove from heat and add most of the coconut, saving some for coating later.

- ➢ Divide the mix into 15 same sized balls.
- ➢ Flatten just enough to wrap around a marshmallow.
- ➢ Encase each marshmallow and then roll in the remaining coconut.

BAKLAVA

Ingredients:

1 and 1/2 pounds chopped walnuts

2 cups sugar

1/2 teaspoon nutmeg

3 teaspoons cinnamon

3 sticks cannabis butter

16 ounces Filo Dough

1 and 1/2 cups water

1 and 1/2 teaspoon lemon juice

2 cups honey

1/2 teaspoon vanilla extract

Directions:

- ➤ Set aside 2 tablespoons of cannabis butter.
- ➤ Use the remaining cannabis butter to grease a 10x15 inch baking dish.
- ➤ Coat 10 sheets of Filo Dough with a layer of butter and place in the baking dish.
- ➤ Mix walnuts with one cup of sugar and pour evenly over the Filo Dough.
- ➤ Butter five more layers of Filo Dough and place in the pan.
- ➤ Preheat oven to 300 degrees.
- ➤ Bake for 50 minutes.
- ➤ In a saucepan; mix remaining sugar, cinnamon, nutmeg, vanilla extract, water and lemon juice.
- ➤ Cook until the mix is syrupy.
- ➤ Add honey and heat for a minute.
- ➤ Remove from heat.
- ➤ Cut into 2x2 inch squares or other desired shape.
- ➤ Pour syrup over Baklava.
- ➤ Set aside for two days to allow the honey to

absorb.

PEANUT BUTTER BALLS

Ingredients:

1 and 1/2 cups peanut butter

1 cup hardened cannabis butter

4 cups powdered sugar

1 and 1/3 cups Graham cracker crumbs

2 cups chocolate chips

1 tablespoon shortening

Directions:

➢ In a large mixing bowl, combine peanut butter and cannabis butter.

➢ Slowly blend in powdered sugar.

➢ Add graham cracker crumbs and mix until stable enough to shape into balls.

➢ Make into 1-inch diameter balls.

➢ In a double boiler, melt chocolate chips and shortening.

➢ Stick a toothpick into each ball and dip them in the chocolate mixture.

➢ Place the balls on a wax paper tray.

➢ Freeze for 30 minutes or until solid.

CHOCOLATE PEANUT BUTTER BARS

Ingredients:

1/2 cup cannabis oil

1/3 cup peanut butter

1 egg

1 cup brown sugar

1 teaspoon vanilla extract

1 cup flour

1 cup chocolate chips

Directions:

➤ Preheat oven to 350 degrees.

➤ Grease a baking pan.

➤ Add cannabis oil, egg, peanut butter, brown sugar and vanilla extra in a bowl and blend until smooth.

➤ Add flour and blend until thoroughly combined.

➤ Add chocolate chips and distribute, so it is evenly spread.

➤ Pour into greased pan and pat to evenly spread.

➤ Bake for 20 to 25 minutes or until a toothpick inserted in center comes out clean.

➤ Once done, cool on wire rack for 30 minutes

before cutting into bars.

CHEX MIX

Ingredients:

6 cups Chex

3/4 cup semi-sweet chocolate

1/3 cup peanut butter

1/4 cup cannabis butter

1/2 teaspoon vanilla extract

1 cup powdered sugar

Directions:

➢ Set aside cereal in a large bowl.

➢ Microwave in 30-second intervals, chocolate, and peanut butter until melted.

➢ Stir in vanilla extract and melted cannabis butter.

➢ Pour chocolate mix over cereal and stir until evenly coated.

➢ Place in large Ziploc bag.

➢ Add powdered sugar to bag and shake until evenly coated.

➢ Store in airtight container in the refrigerator.

DARK CHOCOLATE PUDDING

Ingredients:

12 ounces dark chocolate chips

4 room temperature eggs

4 teaspoons melted cannabis butter

2 teaspoons vanilla extract

Pinch of salt

1 cup boiling hot coffee

Directions:

➢ Combine chocolate chips, eggs, cannabis butter, vanilla extract and salt in a blender.

➢ Pulse a few times to break the chocolate into pieces.

➢ Pour in hot coffee.

➢ Blend at low speed for 2 minutes until smooth.

➢ Pour mixture into pudding bowls.

➢ Refrigerate for 3 hours.

➢ Can be stored in the refrigerator for up to 5 days.

FRUITY RICE CRISPY TREATS

Ingredients:

1.2 ounces strawberries

1.2 ounces blueberries

1.2 ounces mangoes

9 cups crisp rice cereal

1/2 cup & 1 tablespoon unsalted butter

3 tablespoons cannabis butter

5 ounces mini marshmallows

Directions:

> Grease a 9-inch square baking dish and line with parchment paper, allowing for 2 inches to hang over each side.
> Pules strawberries until dust in a blender.
> Transfer strawberries to a medium bowl.
> In the clean blender repeat the process with the blueberries and mangoes, placing each in their own medium bowl.
> Add 3 cups of cereal to each bowl and toss to coat with fruit.
> Melt the unsalted butter and cannabis butter in a small saucepan over medium-low heat.
> Gradually add marshmallows, stirring until combined and melted.
> Divide the marshmallow mixture into the three bowls, stirring well to combine.
> Press the strawberry layer into the baking dish by hand.
> Follow this by the blueberry and mango layers.
> Set at room temperature for 30 minutes.

> Remove from baking dish and cut into squares.

COOKIE DOUGH

Ingredients:

3 tablespoons cannabis coconut oil

1/2 cup peanut butter

1/2 cup ripe, mashed banana

3/4 cup flour

2 tablespoons sugar

1/4 teaspoon cinnamon

1 and 1/2 teaspoon vanilla extract

2 tablespoons milk

1/4 cup mini chocolate chips

Directions:

> Add cannabis coconut oil, peanut butter, mashed banana, sugar, cinnamon, and vanilla to a medium bowl; fully combine with a wooden spoon.
> Stir and incorporate the flour in 1/4 cup intervals until the mixture thickens.
> Add milk until moistened into a smooth cookie dough.
> Stir in chocolate chips.

- Eat as is or freeze as balls for 2 hours to overnight.
- Store in airtight container in the freezer for 2 weeks.

VANILLA CUSTARD

Ingredients:

1 cup cannabis milk

1 cup thickened cream

1 teaspoon vanilla extract

4 egg yolks

1 tablespoon corn flour

1/3 cup caster sugar

Directions:

- In a small saucepan, combine cannabis milk and cream.
- Add vanilla extract and place over medium heat.
- Cook for 5 minutes, stirring constantly.
- Remove from heat.
- In a heatproof bowl; whisk egg yolks, corn flour, and sugar until well combined.
- Pour hot milk mix over egg mix and whisk constantly.

- ➤ Return to saucepan over low heat.
- ➤ Cook for 15 to 20 minutes, stirring constantly or until custard thickens and coats the metal spoon.
- ➤ Serve warm or cold with your choice of garnishment.

DONUTS

Ingredients:

3/4 cup cannabis flour

1/4 cup pastry flour

1 teaspoon baking powder

1/2 cup sugar

1 teaspoon cinnamon

1/2 teaspoon salt

3 tablespoons butter

1/2 cup cannabis milk

1 teaspoon vanilla extract

1 beaten egg

1/2 cup powdered sugar

Directions:

- ➢ Preheat oven to 350 degrees.
- ➢ Cream together sugar and butter.
- ➢ Add the cannabis milk, vanilla extract, and egg; stir until combined.
- ➢ Mix in the cannabis flour, pastry flour, and baking powder.
- ➢ Add cinnamon and salt; mix well.
- ➢ Spoon into greased doughnut pan, filling each segment about 3/4 full.
- ➢ Bake 5 to 9 minutes or until light golden brown.
- ➢ Cool for 5 minutes before removing from pan.
- ➢ Roll in the desired topping.

CARAMEL CORN

Ingredients:

12 cups popped popcorn

1/2 cup cannabis butter

1 cup packed light brown sugar

1/4 cup cannabis honey or corn syrup

2 tablespoons distilled water

1/2 tablespoon salt

1/4 teaspoon baking soda

1/2 teaspoon vanilla extract

Directions:

➢ Preheat oven to 300 degrees.

➢ Grease baking sheets and line with foil.

➢ Spread popcorn on the baking sheets.

➢ In a saucepan over medium heat; combine cannabis butter, brown sugar, cannabis honey or corn syrup, water, and salt.

➢ Bring mixture to a boil while constantly stirring.

➢ Continue to stir for 10 minutes.

➢ Remove from heat.

➢ Stir in baking soda and vanilla extract.

➢ Carefully pour over popcorn and gently mix until well coated.

➢ Bake for 15 to 20 minutes, tossing every 5 minutes.

➢ Remove from oven and allow to cool.

➢ Break up popcorn and store in airtight container.

CHOCOLATE PUDDING

Ingredients:

2 large egg whites

10 tablespoons unsweetened cocoa

2 tablespoons cornstarch

2 and 1/4 cups whole milk

2 to 3 tablespoons melted cannabis butter

1/2 cup sugar

1 teaspoon vanilla extract

Raspberries or other preferred fruit for garnish

Directions:

- ➢ Lightly beat egg whites.
- ➢ In a medium bowl, combine cocoa and cornstarch.
- ➢ Whisk in 1 cup of milk until smooth.
- ➢ Heat remaining milk, cannabis butter and sugar; constantly whisking until it just begins to boil.
- ➢ Reduce heat and simmer for 2 to 3 minutes.
- ➢ Add cocoa mixture and return to heat; simmering again and whisking constantly.
- ➢ Remove from heat and allow to cool for 10 minutes.
- ➢ Add one cup of cocoa mixture to egg whites, whisk and return to pan.
- ➢ Cook on low and don't allow to boil.
- ➢ Remove from heat and stir in vanilla.
- ➢ Allow cooling again.

- ➢ After it reaches room temperature, place in refrigerator.
- ➢ Serve with fruit garnish of your choice.

RICE CRISPY TREATS

Ingredients:

1/4 cup of cannabis butter

5 cups of crisped rice cereal

4 cups of mini marshmallows

Directions:

- ➢ In a large saucepan over low heat slowly melt the cannabis butter.
- ➢ Add the mini marshmallows and stir until melted and well mixed.
- ➢ Cook 2 minutes while stirring constantly.
- ➢ Remove from heat.
- ➢ Add cereal and stir until well coated.
- ➢ Press the mixture into a greased 9x13 inch pan.
- ➢ Allow to cool and then cut into squares.

CINNAMON ROLLS

Ingredients:

Dough:

3 cups cannabis flour

3 tablespoons sugar

1 teaspoon salt

2 teaspoons yeast

1/2 cup cannabis milk

3 tablespoons melted butter

1 egg

Filling:

1/4 cup softened cannabis butter

1/2 cup packed brown sugar

2 tablespoons cinnamon

Icing:

1/4 cup room temperature cream cheese

1 cup powdered sugar

1/4 cup melted cannabis butter

1/2 teaspoon vanilla extract

Directions:

> In a large bowl; mix 2 and 1/2 cups of cannabis flour, sugar, salt, and yeast. Set aside.
> In a separate bowl; combine the cannabis milk and melted butter.
> Add the milk and flour mixture and combine.
> Add the egg.
> Start mixing the last 1/2 cup of cannabis flour, but only enough to make a soft dough.
> Knead the dough for 5 minutes on a floured surface.
> Set dough aside in a lightly greased bowl for 15 minutes.
> Roll out the dough on a floured surface into a 9x13 inch rectangle.
> Spread 1/4 cup of softened cannabis butter on top of the dough.
> Sprinkle cinnamon and brown sugar on top.
> Roll lengthwise into a spiral log.
> Slight evenly into 10 to 12 pieces and place in 9-inch round greased pan.

- ➢ Cover with aluminum foil and allow to rise for 1 hour.
- ➢ Preheat oven to 375 degrees.
- ➢ Bake 20 to 25 minutes or until lightly browned.
- ➢ For the frosting; mix cream cheese, powdered sugar, melted cannabis butter and vanilla extract until smooth.
- ➢ Remove cinnamon rolls from oven and immediately spread with frosting.

BROWNIES

PUMPKIN POT BROWNIES

Ingredients:

2/3 cup packed brown sugar

1/2 cup canned pumpkin

1 egg

2 egg whites

1/4 cup cannabis butter

1 cup flour

1 teaspoon baking powder

1 teaspoon unsweetened cocoa powder

1/2 teaspoon cinnamon

1/2 teaspoon allspice

1/4 teaspoon salt

1/4 teaspoon nutmeg

1/3 cup miniature chocolate pieces

Directions:

➢ Preheat oven to 350 degrees.

➢ Combine brown sugar, pumpkin, egg, egg whites and oil in a large mixing bowl.

➢ Beat on medium speed until well blended.

➢ Add flour, baking powder, cocoa powder, cinnamon, allspice, salt, and nutmeg.

➢ Beat on low until smooth.

➢ Stir in chocolate pieces.

➢ Grease 7x11 inch pan.

➢ Pour batter into the pan, spreading evenly.

➢ Bake 15 to 20 minutes or until a toothpick inserted in the center comes out clean.

OREO BROWNIES

Ingredients:

1 package fudge brownie mix

1/4 cup water

1/2 cup softened cannabis butter

2 eggs

7 coarsely crumbled Oreo cookies

1/2 cup powdered sugar

2 to 4 teaspoons milk

Directions:

- ➢ Preheat oven to 350 degrees.
- ➢ Grease 9x13 inch pan.
- ➢ Stir brownie mix, water, cannabis butter and eggs until well blended.
- ➢ Pour into prepared pan.
- ➢ Sprinkle Oreo cookies over batter.
- ➢ Bake 28 to 30 minutes or until a toothpick inserted in the center comes out clean.
- ➢ Cool completely.
- ➢ Stir powdered sugar and milk until smooth enough to drizzle over brownies.

CHOCOLATE CHERRY BROWNIES

Ingredients:

3/4 cup cannabis butter

6 ounces chopped unsweetened chocolate

2 and 1/2 cups sugar

4 eggs

1 egg yolk

1 and 1/2 teaspoons vanilla extract

1/2 teaspoon almond extract

1 cup and 2 tablespoons flour

1 teaspoon cinnamon

1 cup halved, dried cherries

1 cup chocolate chips

Directions:
- ➢ Preheat oven to 350 degrees.
- ➢ Grease 9x13 inch pan.
- ➢ Melt cannabis butter over low heat in heavy saucepan.
- ➢ Add unsweetened chocolate and stir until smooth.
- ➢ Remove from heat and mix in sugar.
- ➢ Add eggs one at a time and then add the egg yolk.
- ➢ Add vanilla and almond extracts, flour and cinnamon; stirring until well blended.
- ➢ Add cherries and chocolate chips.
- ➢ Pour batter into the pan.
- ➢ Bake for 35 minutes or until a toothpick inserted in the center comes out clean.
- ➢ Allow cooling.

HONEY CHOCOLATE BROWNIES

Ingredients:

1 cup melted cannabis butter or oil

1/2 cup melted unsweetened chocolate or cocoa powder

4 eggs

1 cup honey

2 teaspoons vanilla extract

2 cups flour

2 teaspoons baking powder

1/2 teaspoon salt

1 cup raisins

1 cup chopped nuts

Directions:

➢ Preheat oven to 350 degrees.

➢ Grease a 9x13 inch pan.

- ➢ Whip butter, chocolate, and honey together until smooth.
- ➢ Add eggs and vanilla extra; mix well.
- ➢ Combine wet and dry ingredients; stir until moist.
- ➢ Add raisins and nuts; mix well.
- ➢ Pour into baking pan.
- ➢ Bake for 45 minutes or until a toothpick inserted in the center comes out clean.

FUDGE NUT BROWNIES

Ingredients:

2 cups chocolate chips

1/4 cup cannabis butter

2 cups biscuit baking mix

1 can sweetened condensed milk

1 beaten egg

1 teaspoon vanilla extract

1 cup coarsely chopped walnuts

Directions:

- ➢ Preheat oven to 350 degrees.
- ➢ Melt 1 cup chocolate chips with cannabis butter over low heat in a large saucepan.
- ➢ Remove from heat.

- ➢ Add biscuit mix, condensed milk, egg and vanilla extract.
- ➢ Stir in nuts and remaining chocolate chips.
- ➢ Pour into greased 9x13 inch baking pan.
- ➢ Bake 20 to 25 minutes or until a toothpick inserted in the center comes out clean.

Appendix A
Making Cannabis Milk

Several of the recipes above talked about cannabis milk. This is one of the less common items you'll make with cannabis unless you are considering some dessert recipes. The following is how you make cannabis milk.

Ingredients:

1 Liter of full-fat milk

25 grams of finely powdered cannabis

Directions:

➢ Using a double boiler, bring milk to a boil and let simmer.

➢ Add cannabis in small amounts while constantly stirring, until the cannabis is entirely covered by the milk.

➢ Simmer for 30 to 45 minutes and stir occasionally.

➢ It is natural for the milk to turn a yellowish-green color.

➢ Remove from heat and strain well with a cheesecloth.

➢ Allow cooling then keep in the refrigerator.

Appendix B
Making Cannabis Corn Syrup

Another less common cannabis preparation you'll need is cannabis corn syrup. A few recipes above called for it so let's look at the process for making it.

Equipment and Ingredients:

Slow cooker

3 glasses light corn syrup

1 ounce finely ground cannabis

Cheesecloth

Spoon

Container

Directions:

➢ Pour light corn syrup into a slow cook or stewing pot. Place on low/medium.

➢ The corn syrup should be hot without bubbling.

➢ Add cannabis.

➢ Blend as often as needed for 4 hours.

➢ Turn off heat and allow it to cool slightly.

➢ Pour corn syrup through a cheesecloth into a container.

➢ Allow syrup to cool.

➢ Store in an airtight container in a cool, dim spot.

Made in the USA
Columbia, SC
05 September 2018